LOTUS under the SUN

Troshell Richardson

Copyright © 2015 by Troshell Richardson. All rights reserved.

Not Just Alphabets Publishing

Fort Worth, Texas

All Troshell Richardson titles, imprints and verses distributed are available at special quantity discounts for bulk purchases for sales promotion, fund raising, premiums, educational, institutional and library use.

Copyright © 2015 by Troshell Richardson. All rights reserved.

No part of this work may be reproduced or transmitted in any form or by any means, electronic or mechanical, including photocopying and recording, or by any information storage retrieval system without the prior written permission of Troshell Richardson unless such copying is expressly permitted by federal copyright law. Email: oasisbreez776@gmail.com to request Permission.

Printed in the U. S. A.

Library of Congress Catalog Card Number:

ISBN: 978-0-9963129-8-1

Dedication:

In loving memory of

Sammie Lorraine Hewitt

Table of Content

Crossroads 6

Maybe Not Forever 9

Here Before 10

Complications 12

Beautiful 14

Her Eyes 15

She 17

To Write Love On Her Arms 18

Awakening 19

Uncharted Waters 20

Spanish Infusion 22

Skin 24

Miss You 26

Breaths of My Heart 27

Innocence 28

Silent Tragedy 32

Heaven 35

Her Thoughts 36

New Beat 38

Naked 41

War Inside 42

Your Body 44

Caught 46

All of You 48

Whisper 50

Scars 51

Silence 53

The Other Side of Lonely 55

The State of Fate 56

Your Fan 58

Artist 59

Red White Blue 62

In You 64

Thank You 65

Acknowledgements 66

Biography 67

Contact Information 68

copyright © 2015 Troshell Richardson all rights reserved

Crossroads

standing at the crossroads

where deals were made for souls

the smell of forever lingers

many a broken dreams lie discarded

like here... is where you better them

where choices come and go

where you can pick the ones

you like best – what price is too high

how much sacrifice is too much

I've heard it was hell or high water

but here there's only light

and arrows pointing in every direction

I am unsure if this is forward

or backward past the beginning

which direction do I lean

no clue of where to go

a choice I used to toss to the wind

there is a force, a tug of war

a constant pulling at my heart

decisions in my yesterday's

once as easy as picking my favorite color

now leaves my mind floating

in the sea of uncertainty

what do I do with this mangled web

of thoughts bouncing around in my head

act on impulse or think it over instead

who will I hurt with this decision

will I find comfort in the confines

of this new space?

or strike another blow to love

rendering it wounded

I've patched these places before

the new space feels so familiar

feels good - as if

it were chosen for me by me

the force grows stronger

pulling at my heart

keeping me from choosing

reality is the mist I feel on my face

as heaven cries – this is the hardest

decision I remember having to make

these crossroads are a myth

no deals to make here

I alone must choose

left or right – forward or back

today is not the day to rest

here choices come and go

how much sacrifice is enough

how much is too much

what is not enough

this new place feels familiar

feels like home away from home

which way to go

is a difficult decision to make

happiness seems so complicated

maybe I will walk slow

for peace seems a long way from here

Maybe Not Forever

there is nothing like sharing

a moment with your ex-lover

you give out, I give in

we tried to make the intimate work

only to discover

love isn't always intimate

sometimes love is just love

our journey started

because you said hello

the sound of happy turned into

everyday conversations

we talked of maybe's

and to be's and wish list

spending time exploring

hoping this is how love looks

we knew trials would come

who knew unknown feelings

would act this way

the forever's we spoke of

was our foundation

we believed eternity was meant to be

I watched as you removed

the armor plating from your heart

I never knew love didn't have hands

didn't need to feel your insides

to live inside of you

thought those lips were mine

forgot they produce the talking

the sounds

the hello

that brought us here

we began as friends

became lovers

thought forever was easy

thought eternities

were in the making

maybe eternity

lies in you and me

being friends

for life

not married

for life

we make our own beliefs

or believe what is made for us

will be for us

what if

friends are better

than lovers

and the trials were lessons

teaching us

there is so much more

to forever than wishing

than wanting

and eternity

lies in you and me

being friends

for life

Here Before

I am convinced

somewhere through the center

of your chest

lives a doorway to me

your eyes pierce my thoughts

as though they see into my soul

your hands held me

like they have been there before

Fate brought us back

this could be our third time around

my body moves to a rhythm

only you can create

we sang a song

we moved in time

danced dances

neither of us knew

I could love you for real

my thoughts moved

to be near the aroma

of your sound

the wind seemed to carry

the essence of your being

It holds me with no respite

your smile mesmerizing

all consuming I felt your teeth

your lips pulling me in

like the lake to the sea

you beach front calmed

my spirit

I lost parts of me

how is it you know my body

so well and you've never touched me

your DNA runs rapid through my veins

a surgical transfusion

was not what

the doctor ordered

I could get used to this

could miss all the places

we haven't been

could wake mornings

missing your presence

missing you being

where you have yet to go

I could get used to closed eye memories

made from sleep, from dreams so real

I beg myself not to wake

It is as if I know things about you

I have yet to ask enough questions to learn

I could get used to this

to distant simultaneous thoughts

to smiling at the same time

to these moments of conscious

of new awakening I find myself discovering

all I said was hello asked how was your day

for days all I could hear was your hello

I could get to this

I could love you for real

Complications of Love

self-preservation is the ability

to hold yourself back

from feeling the right now

from rushing head first

into ecstasy's arms

it will seem real

I want to believe it's real

past experience's

keeps my heart corralled

how does one come back

from being shunned aside

while the "other" takes a ride

thought you had a love

endless and so deep

you almost felt you would die

if their love you couldn't keep

love is such a complex word

most are still trying

to discover it's meaning

It is described as a feeling

of euphoria and bliss

Love is so slow to come

you keep reaching out

pressing for its presence

and one day tomorrow's here

not the one you prayed for

not the great one

you thought would come

I search myself

and love remains absent

love is as complicated

as hanging fresh mistletoe

on Easter

as wishing for

instead of working towards

I offered my best kisses

surrendered my favorite smile

why won't love return?

I've found lost images

of love's silhouette

abandoned in the shade

hiding in the corners

of this mind

behind the drums

in these ears

I can see hear and taste love

long after she appears

on milk cartons

long after one set of prints

rest gently on the sands

alone isn't a song

anyone wants to dance to

love is complex

complicated

the reason we cry

our source of laughter

Beautiful

B- beyond

E- exterior

A- additives

U-utilizing

T- the

I- inner

F- fire

U - under

L- what Lies beneath

Beauty

is not

only outside

looks will fade

it is comprised

of the inside

as well

let's let our

inner beauty

shine through

Her Eyes

her eyes

her eyes have a story

inside her eyes lies the hurt

and pain that came

with having to suffer

hiding the whys

the how comes

her eyes have a story

are you the one

to look deep within

to discover what unfolds

she speaks volumes

with the deep hue

of brown eyes

she has labored

for what seems eternally in vain

reaching out pulling back

an empty hand

her eyes have a story

who will hold her up

for she stands strong

for everyone else

she encompasses all

a woman of strength could entail

she walks with a smile on her face

while inside she screams

her eyes have a story

she had no listening ear

from the ones she feels

should have her back

she gives to those who don't deserve her gifts

though with kindness she continues

her eyes have a story

she gives of herself

almost to the point of empty

who will fill her again

prayer you think would be the logical answer

though flesh doesn't think so

her eyes have a story

look into her eyes they tell her history

working hard for what is important

though the importance seems oblivious

to the pain that is building

the feeling of lagging behind

her eyes have a story

do you want to know her story

or is this where you close the book

put it back on the shelf

her eyes need someone to peer in

and see she looks for no handout

just the ability to be recognized

for her effort

her eyes have a story

peer in, be serious about your intention

for her eyes tell a story

they need to be heard

are you ready to listen

SHE

SHE IS

thoughts that drip

from my lips

when I think about

what SHE is to me

If you sit and listen

I'll grant you first class

listening admission

SHE is who I want

desire, crave and dream about

SHE makes me smile

at the mere calling of her name

SHE listens to my thoughts

I have and the ones

I don't speak about

SHE is my muse

SHE is my good thing

I see my future in her eyes

no longer will I compromise

my happiness for the happiness

of someone else

my poetry speaks about her

SHE is my smile

SHE makes life and breathing worth while

SHE is the grace in my walk

and the calm in my sleep

SHE is who makes my life

completely amazing

To Write Love On Her Arms

the scars of yesterday still fresh

open wounds make my heart hurt

my need is to write her love

messages so she could see

in the most important places

pain often goes unspoken

lips closed tight as I hear her scream

silence has never been so loud

If only I could write love on her lips

the color of joy

whisper love to her mind

drenched in remembrance

paint love in the curve of her spine

my need is to write her love

a language of which few are familiar

my tongue speaks it fluently

if only I could kiss love in her eyes

allowing her vision to grasp

don't know if she can see me

singing love, resuscitating feelings lying

dormant since the last invasion

I wish to squeeze love in her bones

hold her so close we may just become one

my need is to write her love

even her arms will know that

around me is how we are supposed

to write this love into Love

Awakening

the ground is breaking

now I'm free

now I can accept

the calling

of the prophetic lyricist

you see

I manipulate the words

as they flow from my pen

I watch them bubble

until they explode

listen to me

if you please

and let me take you

on a journey

I will share my world

my inner soul

how I got over life's

blunders and blows

through the sharing

of my words

I have gained new meaning of life

through the words

I have awakened a part of my soul

I never new existed

I have embodied

the personification of me

this is the awakening

of my life's greatest work

Uncharted Waters

I am on a soul quest

to find my best living

in the in-between

of unresolved healing

I have entered this journey

to find the real meaning

sentenced to an emotional

sexual and spiritual detox

standing on the shore

waiting for the sunrise

to appear over the horizon

praying to God above

through healing

I will gain peace

from the hurt places to speak

asking for spiritual guidance

sanctifying my heart and mind

realizing that what I thought

was fear was only catalyst

to the healing space of completeness

no this is not my destiny

this is a time my history

to get to the place

of certainty and wholeness

that I may stand boldly

as a Nubian queen

of my lineal decent

fate will let the test of time

determine what it may be

I am a rare jewel

seeking her rightful place

in this world

no longer accepting meritocracy

I need something more genuine

not just circumstantial

on a soul quest to find

who Troshell R. really is

what's beneath the hue

of her brown eyes

why they have cried

many nights to find out why

this wont be easy

this is for sure

but to find my wholeness

I must endure

endure the pain of places

never delved before

why I couldn't come

with my whole self

why I had to send my representative

fearful that no one would

love me completely all of me

am I a damaged soul

questions indeed

I will uncover in the quest

for my spirit and soul

Spanish Infusion

her fingers

must have known

me from before

maybe Cruzan rum

or mescal from Mexico

she played me

a song with strings

I danced

as I listened

the exotic sounds

filled the air

dancing

a sensual samba

cascading sounds

rise and fall

as the strings

are being strummed

in a melodious symphony

it plays

a song of love

never conceived before

I close my eyes

to the sound

of the calypso beat

my heart

became as thin

as the strings

playing my life's notes

I must have

Ecuador in my linage

or Guatemala

in my belly

serenading me

to a place

of clear skies

oceans so blue

I could feel

the warm sun

beating down

against my caramel

colored skin

reflecting

secret parts of me

rays of rhythms

to this soul of mine

pulling me in

and letting me go

I moved as though

I were the dance

itself

a derivative of

ancestral courtship

Skin

I want to feel your skin

invite me into you

tantalizing the epidermis of your being

canvasing your body slowly

imprinting my fingerprints in your DNA

this time loving you

not in the physical

but in the metaphysical

cosmos being created in new galaxies

passions heated watching your silhouette

by warm candlelight

anticipation to render your body

with slow deserving praise

is becoming harder to hold back

though I don't want to rush

I want to take it slowly

love you boldly

controlling the very way

you come to me

I wanna wear your skin

not literally

but feel how you feel

if I could be inside of you

not physically

but become your veins

feel how they travel through

the soul of you

I want our breath

to be

as if god made us

there is no you and I

just us

we

I have a dream

every dream

I dream of you

dreamed everything

I could do to you

I wish to take this slowly

make you feel

you belong to me

belong inside these arms

resting your head

on my pillows of wisdom

allowing complete

peace to reside

creating something

so sublime

if you let me

show you

Miss You

I miss the tenderness in your touch

I miss the passion in your love

I miss the sweetness in your voice

I miss the closeness we once shared

the laughter that once filled our lives

is now consumed with questions and whys

I meander from day to day

trying to believe all this is worth it,

though the path in which we are on,

gives me reason to doubt it

my heart aches in a way

I never thought possible

the once sweet phrase

I love you

is now filled with hurt.

there is no joy to be found

lingering in the words

that seep from your lips

there was a time I could see

myself in your eyes

I now question my existence in your world

so I ask myself

what must I do to get you back

I want to give you a safe haven to come to

I want to care for you, hold you

erase the fears that consume you

allow me to be your comfort

I miss you

Breaths of My Heart

smoke screens

and alluded dreams

of what we think love should be

sweet kisses caught up in bliss

Is where we think love should stay

while facing adversity

and conflict in love

then the hard times come

and the first thought is to run

because the once tangible love

is no longer there.

so how do you reach a love

that seems unreachable

how do you touch a love

that seems untouchable

what do you use as an anchor

while the world blows up around you

how do get love back

that seems to be slowly drifting away

how do you smile

while your eyes fill with tears

and emotions never experienced

are all over the place

how do you continue

to tell yourself everything will be okay

when your the reason it got this way

these are the thoughts of a hurting soul

Innocence

innocence Slain

because she was given

a misconstrued meaning of life

though life was lived out

in front of her by what she knew

to be as a husband and wife.

people who have been appointed

to give guidance and love.

through their actions showed none of the above

a mother who didn't care

to see that innocence

was truly hurting deep within

and daddy

well daddy was to busy

trying to get in between

not between the one he was married to

but in between innocence

who had no fight

and the one who was having the life

sucked right out of her

she was given

the definition of her life

you'll never amount to anything

she takes this and starts acting as such

who would love her

broken and abused

so she walks around like she has no worth

all because her future

was being prematurely birthed

she was sentenced to death

long before her life could take flight

who would see that she had so much to offer

a talented artist and writer

she was a walking miracle

to say the least

coming from a background

of beatings and fatherly nighttime creeps

she asked herself the question

why me?

she feels that she should suppress

the femininity of being

a beautiful Nubian queen

she takes on a whole new persona

becoming what wont get her noticed or seen

you see being beautiful

is what brought all the negativity it seems

she is an adult now,

and though she has moved on

she still carries the burden

the scars deep within

she has a child of her own

vows she will always protect and show love

be the best mother she could be

she didn't want to bring her child

into the hell she was brought up in

she moves and it seems

a better life has begun

though there's one thing missing

from this new life

love

she has encounters that seemed to fit

the one thing she had desired

family and a wife

but soon their veils were lifted

their representatives left

their real identities showed up

she then realized she needed

to possibly start with finding self

maybe she is the reason

love had not come for her

she knew one thing

she desired love

needed love

in her quest she found

she needed not to find love in others

she had to first find love in herself

she prayed and fasted

she went on this healing journey

to find love and her acceptance

of her renewed self

she wanted wholeness

mind, body, and soul

It was revealed the next person

to have her heart

would have to prove themselves

worthy enough

God had a plan

he was preparing someone

who would hear her plea

and they were ready to prove

themselves worthy

they were there waiting

to stick it through

thick and thin

all because they loved her

wholeheartedly

no fillers or schemes

she says to herself

is this it?

could it really be

someone is here

to love me

just for me

did they really want to see

her broken heart

was riddled with scars

did they come to heal

not to tear apart

though frightened

and confused

she opened the door

of love once more

and she finally had

her love eternal

Silent Tragedy

silent cry's

come from black

and blue eyes

all the while wearing

the cloak of this thing

called love

she humbles herself

thinking it will lesson the blows

that ramble her soul

like a 10.0 earthquake

she feels as if she can just behave

at least that's what Mr. says

things wouldn't be this way

silent cry's

while she try's

to hide the pain and anguish

going on inside

she smiles

to somehow hide the guilt

the shame that has made her

scared to leave

the silent cry's

in the middle of the night

wanting to know

if the fight will be her last

as he beats her senseless

she is loosing consciousness

he sees what he's doing

and he lets go

gifts shadow the room

attached to a thank you

I'll never do it again

she questions is this truly

what love is supposed to be.

as moments pass and eternity

doesn't look so promised

days become hours

hours become minutes

and minutes become seconds

she knows she has to break free

her heart begins to cringe

because she feels her fate

coming to an end

she cant seem to understand

why the man that claims

I'm his queen

why does he continue to beat me

no longer can she hide

black and blue eyes

with the superficial

covers of makeup

her cry's are no longer silent

she needs help

who will come through

for they see her eyes

are black and blue to

will they not get involved

and result to ignorance

saying child its not my problem

he is good man

a girl gotta do

what she has to do

or will someone come boldly

and offer me a way of escape

well you would say

if she gets tired

she will leave

that maybe true

though the blackened eyes

and the silent cry's

the fear inside

keep her here

no one comes

they don't see

this could be their mother

sister or daughter

so they again say

its not my problem

and what could have been changed

has now become

a silent tragedy

because death was her fate

Heaven

tempt me with your kiss

captivate me with your touch

engage my every thought

with your presence

that i desire so much

I have a situation

come without hesitation

come to the position

that commands me

to give full submission

entangle your wetness

into my sweetness

and devour my flower

swallowing all of its juices

flowing from my desire

with each flick of your tongue

my legs began to quake

from the bliss I'm in

you put your fingers inside me

and make me cum again and again

you put me out in ecstasy

not sure of how much I can take

you whisper real sweet I'm going deep

I scream out your name

there's no place I'd rather be

than right here

you and me

loving together endlessly

Her Thoughts

when she's sleep

you wonder the thoughts she keeps

you wonder how you can keep the purity within

from the rise and fall

of her calling for deeper rest

you caress her face and pull her close

you feel there is no place

you would rather be

when she sleeps

you wonder the thoughts she keeps

you see a strong woman

all she has endured you admire her strength

though your saddened

because she has not been able

to be vulnerable

you have this protection mode for her

wanting to keep her in safety

having no worry or fear

you see the fragile part of her

and want to nurture it

you caress her with the softest touch

the sweetest kiss

and the longest embrace

you make this love worth having

when she sleeps

you wonder the thoughts she keeps

you wonder if she is Happy in this place

you know her past

you want to enhance her future

make her dreams reality

you can feel her near

her head nestled in your chest

all peaceful and serene

yet in some way

this doesn't seem real

your waiting for the dream to be over

though we desire it

nothing sometimes is what it seems

when she's sleep

you wonder the thoughts she keeps

you wonder if she is in it just as much as you

you wonder if she will have the power

to withstand what may come through

you want to know if the love

and passion she implodes is for keeps

with this thought you pull her close

almost inside your skin

inhaling the vanilla scent of her embodiment

so you think in your thoughts

and pray real hard you don't fall

victim to circumstance

you want all of this is for you

you look at her

kiss her passionately and say to yourself

I'm here and will give you all I got

you breathe and let go

although you wonder thoughts she keeps

New Beat

loving the way you caress the words

flowing from your heart to your pen

awaiting the time I can pledge

until there's No more giving

you are all I want

I'm open

I dance

I write

contemplating the future

you caress my heart

as you lyrically make love

to it's beating rhythm

making it your own

I dance

I write

I now dance to a beat

that was mine

even before time was time

you are the perfect resemblance

of what my mind felt love should be

do you hear the beat of the drum

rhythm heard by none

It's the only beat

I want to put lyrics to forever

I dance

I write

when I hear the beat of the bass

my heart sings and skips a beat

I can hardly speak

my body moves

in a way yet discovered

nor seen by any

I dance

I write

I question whether it's real

although when I smell your scent

feel your breath on my neck

your touch and embrace

I am sunk back into reality

that this is for me

I applaud all my hurts

disappointments, heartache

and pain, because

had none of that been

I wouldn't have found this beat

this chain of rhythms

cords crescendos, bravados

my lyrics come alive

and I have new meaning to a love

I didn't feel I could achieve

and for the first time

with all the beats I've danced to

I finally found

a beat I could speak to

I dance

I write

you caress my mind

speak volumes

to my heart

so I dance

I write

I wake up

in a new light

that warms me

with No respite.

your beat has me open

unable to control the dance

that spills forth

and I never knew

loves door could be so giving

enchanting, engaging

all these amazing things

so

I dance

I write

I completely lay down

the loss of faith

in love

and I dance

and I write

to the new beat

of my drum

Naked

take off your clothes

let me unveil you

with my eyes

drifting into the abyss

of your eternity

caressing your body

with thoughts

of what I want

to do to you

wanting to engage your senses

feel your energy

allowing a cosmic collision

to take place

feeling your skin

the heat it gives

my energy

pulling you in

for a catastrophic explosion

of feelings to take over

no need for words

lets allow the presence

of us do the talking

I want to know

every square inch

of your masterpiece

and to think,

I haven't even touched you yet

I haven't even touched you yet

War Inside

always laughing

to keep from crying

her appearance

doesn't mirror

the battle raging inside

she smiles as though pain

comes with a hint of joy

hidden in the day to day

struggle life demands

you look at her and think

a model citizen for happy

she has it all together

able to withstand

all types of weather

you would never see

the scrimp and save

the robbing Peter

to pay Paul

the sacrifices

to care for her young

she prays for this days strength

her face hides traces of tears

a pillows song at midnight

some days

she grips time tightly

hoping to hold it still

a twist and turn

of minutes

needing a moment

to gather herself

even if you asked

you couldn't tell

if the good

wasn't great

and the great

wasn't better

she wears burdens

as designer clothes

a heart full of love

no one would know

the war inside

is real

her smile is too

she has grown accustomed

to doing whatever

she has to do

you would look at her

and think

she has it all together

able to withstand

through all types of weather

Your Body

my body

still remembers

your touch

my senses still react

to the all to familiar sent

I still remember

the late night visits

bestowing priceless gifts

my lips still taste your kiss

you are etched in my spirit

I try and shake the feeling

of wanting to be apart

of your life in an intimate way

just when I think

I have a handle on the situation

thoughts of you, us

bombard my thinking

enjoying the time we spend

still I crave more

my conscious tells me

to just let go

though I don't want

to drift to far off

maybe its a test of will

to see if I really have

the will to endure

my lips speak about you

how do I put things

in perspective and still

keep what we have

what we are building

stability

firm foundation

thoughts of my heart

Caught

don't want to be

caught up in you

the way you walk

talk and smile boo

I don't want to be

caught up in you

I've got to break

these chains that keep

wanting to call you

I don't want to be

caught up in you

but when I hear your name

it has me smiling for you

I don't want to be

caught up in you

you call me

I get weak in the knees

what is it about you

I can not let go

what is about you

leaves me wanting more

I don't want to be

caught up in you

Is it your swagger

how you wear your clothes

I don't know

I don't want to be

caught up in you

you fill me

full of empty promises

empty love

what is about this love

I can not deviate from

instead of you showering

your love down on me

all you do is fill me

full of misery

so today my dear

I'm breaking the chains

binding me to you

and you no longer have

the black cloud

over my heart

All of You

I want all of you

even the parts of you

you've hidden from you

use your imagination

on how you want this be

let's explore each other

leave the fantasy

for children's tales

I want all of you

release your mind to me

open your chest

I will build a new future

from the fragments

of your past

let me open doors

no one else knew

how to open before

I want to explore

what makes you laugh

the origin of your sad

where the water

for your tears

come from

what makes you smile

I want all of you

I want to

awaken your soul

from the abyss

bring it to the light

give it peace

I want to invigorate

your skin

let me pleasure

your senses

again and again

I want all of you

even the parts you

you thought were lost

let me be the sun

that awakens your day

the moon above your bed

your comforter

to keep you warm

I want all of you

I want more

not just your body

I want to know you

inside and out

take me into your world

captivate my senses

bring me to submission

I want all of you

Whisper

a soft whisper

delicate kisses

upon my lips

you engage my attention

with your eloquent

way of speaking

I anticipate your hands

canvassing my body

pulling out

all that has been

waiting for you

your warm breath

cascades over my face

instantly

making my mouth water

you step closer

making the wetness

between my thighs

impossible to bare

please release me

from this agony

of wanting to shower you

in my sweet nectar

you pull me close

no way to break free

and we get tangled

in our love fantasy

Scars

the scars that comes from life's

disappointments and mistakes

I used to stand in the stands

of my affliction

somethings holding me

with no escape

how could I redeem myself

from my mistakes

the people I let down

I attempted to keep

the scars away

smiling, though my stains

were starting to seep through

the ability to hide them

became impossible to do

I was encompassed

in my thoughts, fears

disappointments

and Lack of understanding

no longer cared about life

nor the things it was demanding

I no longer appreciated life

and wanted it to end

I didn't have the guts

to take my own life

so my solution

to life's problems lived

 in the vice of the bottle

this endless elixir seemed

to fill my doubts and my fears

though it was sending me

into a whirlwind of emotions

and uncontrollable tears

I would go too far

as my realities

seemed to dissipate

the more I drank

felt myself drifting

into the sea

of an endless abyss

life was spinning

out of control

my life was on the line

but God whispered sweetly

in my ear

in the midst of my mess

and He said

you have purpose

you are worthy

you are healed

and redeemed

God covered me

in His Grace

He lifted me

no longer do I hide

in the shadows of my scars

for I am free

Silence

silence was something

I could never embrace

I could never find comfort

in the nothingness

of movement and time

I easily accept chaos

surround myself with

the hustle and bustle of life

the non-movement of silence

is overwhelming loud and frightening

the thought of getting lost in myself

in the past I hold like future

is not what I wanted

I believe in the spirit of quiet

in the comfort of noise

I place my thoughts in

this time silence is inevitable

I sent it a personal invitation

made reservations for dinner

dressed silence in formal wear

we will dine in the elegant setting

of no one but I - me

I want it here - I need it

I have faith if I get to know

its origin - if I learn

the sound of my own footsteps

practice smacking I've forgotten how

teach myself the funny I lost

redraw my smile

from inside out

discover the reasons I have

rejected our union for so long

I've heard there is a hidden code

only silence knows

you can only find there

I never wanted to be

in close proximity

of memories I wished away

of the times I let me down

arms failing from the weight

of holding someone else up

reaching stars I saw my name on

I need to feel how it feels

to hold me

to catch myself

I may practice falling

to get used to

catching myself

silence was always the one thing

I was afraid to touch

afraid to let it find me

without the noise

I used for comfort

now I welcome its company

I have silence on speed dial

soon we will dine - we will feast

just silence and I

The Other Side of Lonely

starting today

I laid down my want

for us to continue

I release you to the place

where you belong

often times hurt and pain

though no longer felt

cause such disappointment

sting lingers longer after its gone

my hope and prayer

for reconciliation

to began was unveiled

although not in the way

I wanted or intended

so I release you

I release the passion

held for you

embrace our inevitability

the other side of lonely

I embrace and embark

on this journey

of loving you intimately

to just loving you

no longer feeling

emotions felt one way

accepting who we are to be entirely

our destiny to be fulfilled all along

The State of Fate

frustration always sets in

not knowing the fate of our young

the random executions of our youth

is becoming far too common

young men fatherless are now fathers

our daughters are missing their childhood

slaying their innocence

our daughters have been taken

hurt and shown so much disdain

we are in a battle, caught in a war

not a war for country but this war

is of our own choosing

caused by the ignorance

polluting their minds

every hot track talking about

snapping it back and the music videos

making it seem if you wear less

you will be considered the best

who will accept the responsibility

for raising the level of integrity

in our young ladies

it is impossible for babies to grow babies

for our babies are having babies

this generations path is no longer paved

with good intentions

or women willing to make a difference

the ones who believe in creating change

or so few or non-existent

our daughters are taught

beauty can be bought

purchased as hair manufactured for resale

lips injected and painted purple or perfect

butts added as if bodies are better than brains

abuse and bullied into believing their voices

are not necessary their sound unaccountable

self-esteem whipped out of them

snuffed out like a forest ablaze

drenched with rain

how will we inspire our daughters

to know greatness rest in their beings

when all they know and see is sorrow

broken men and broken hearts

every song singing of broken parts

mothers and daughters are friends

the boundaries are crossed

it is impossible for babies to grow babies

for our babies are having babies

these are the girls who will soon be women

the leaders, the matriarchs, the Rosa Parks

the conquerors of our tomorrows

we must teach them of the love inside

that happy resides in their smiles

to have belief in themselves

teach them of integrity

it begins with us displaying

proving we are the queen of this domain

and show them what integrity looks like

Your Fan

even though

we are not what we used to be

I still feel you

your invigorating

and intoxicating smell

still surrounds me

the essence of your memory

still pricks at my soul

with each melody of songs

I sing of songs that encompassed

our relationship

you are the gem worthy of

the perfect box

wrapped in a precious exotic satin

worthy of the softest touch

though we may never be again

I hold you in the terrace

of my heart

for you were my love

my sexy

my exotic

don't loose your glow

for you are

and forever will be loved

by me in the shadows

of the stands

for I will always be

your biggest fan

Artist

different is an

understatement

I have grown accustomed

to the usual

to thinking dreaming

means asleep

and dreams

take form on their own

I have watched wind

become pages

and pages transform

into canvases

I wasn't aware pens

brushes and fingers

were one and the same

I sit watching

to see what unfolds

Paper

Charcoal

Your hands

you formulate a masterpiece

I'm checking you out

allowing art to create

something never seen

your love for the arts

exploding on canvas

me writing what I see

transcribing in words

I often see me in the lines

feel my breath in verses

you still mesmerize me

how you take

what seemingly

looks innocent

like it's lesson

has been lost

thinking nothing

of these nothings

and a vision is formed

Paper

Charcoal

Your hands

a gift from God

given to a queen

perfected by experience

I love watching you

make images come to life

Paper

Charcoal

Your hands

I thought once I saw

or read your fingers sign

as if I could read braille

or knew how alphabets

sounded in the wind

I thought I watched

you write a miracle

or was it a song

it could have been

the rain falling

Paper

Charcoal

Your Hands

remind me of scriptures

how talents given

must be grown

how God allows

us one gift

to spawn many givers

Paper

Charcoal

Your hands

my thoughts and fingers

are drafting miracles now

I wrote a prayer in a poem

a gift in a note

I think therefore I be

blessed also

with

Paper

Charcoal

Hands

and God

He made me

a Poet

Red White Blue

my hands are up

not armed at all

so stop don't shoot

we don't need the attack dogs

shot and killed with no remorse at all

thought he was holding

was the excuse given as a cause

why I let off 5 rounds

and watched him fall

red white and blue

laid me out

in cold blood

for the world to see

senseless acts with no thought at all

just another one of our black men gone

what happened to serve and protect

red white and blue

killing young black men

who are no threat

murders taken place in all states

police handing out the black man's fate

fear being filled in the hollows

of our young men's hearts

and what do we say to them

to make them feel alright

this is truly slavery at its best

red white and blue

you're doing it all wrong

no need to aim and kill

give our black men

the chance to live

I will agree no crime

should not go unpunished

but a hooded teen

with tea and skittles

does not fit the bill

shooting 12 rounds

to an assumption

is not a defense

to the defenseless

masking a babies face

as innocent as they come

what did she do wrong?

where was her crime from

we need to stand

and put an end

to this madness and mayhem

we are living in a sick world

where life is not valued

red white and blue

attacking the elderly

and the mentally ill

we have stand for what's right

until justice is carried through

or these heinous crimes

will continue

In You

I want to live

inside your poem

live inside the words

you don't speak

live inside

the words that come

from your pen filled with love and pain

I want to bask inside thoughts

created and poured onto pages

nouns, verbs,

similes and metaphors

conveyed with truth

a melody of choreographed syllables

no one puts together like you

I want to live inside your poem

carried away into a sea of your vocabulary

exploring its vast terrain of hyperboles

carried by commas and periods

want to feel the drop in your heart line

read a thought that made you smile

I want to loose myself inside your poem

feel the highs and lows that rise and fall

I want to live inside your definition of love

please

let

me

live

inside your poem

Thank you for your support

Acknowledgements

I dedicate this book to for and fore most God for Blessing me with this gift. I also want to thank my mother for cultivating my gift. I want to thank my friends for pushing me, even I didn't want to be pushed. I want to thank Houston for his tireless effort in helping me with this project. A special thank you to Abebi Ekundayo for her encouragement.

BIOGRAPHY

Troshell Richardson was born in Inglewood, California, she moved to Dallas while still a toddler. Her mother and father both live in the Dallas area, her one sibling a sister lives on the east coast. She began writing at an early age, in the beginning she only wrote out of anger. Troshell discovered at the start of moving her pen it was the perfect tool to use as an emotional outlet. You would seldom see her without a book in her possession, reading was one of the things she loved. Expressing herself through writing was how she journeyed through school. When she went to live with her grandmother who was a journalist for one of the local papers in Dallas, Texas the Post Tribune at age sixteen she began writing again. She has continued to this day to scribe her thoughts and emotions on paper. When her uncle pasted away, she wrote a poem to pay homage after presenting it to the family one of her aunts told her the poem was really good and she felt there is true talent in her writing. She started taking writing as a serious endeavor after hearing the words of support by signing up for a few writing classes. At this point there will be no stopping her from finding better and more interesting ways to say what she must say through the art of poetry. She is the mother of three... Kaylon 19, Mikayla 16 and Tia 10. Troshell now residing in Fort Worth, Texas frequent a lot of the Speak Easy's in the DFW Metroplex area. You can hear her on the mic from Dallas to Fort Worth and everything in between. Her belief when asked about life was "I look over my life's past and realize that all of my heart aches and difficult times were presented to make me stronger. They were struggles just for me. I breathe writing. It enhances who I am. The ink flows none stop and I have learned to reach places in my heart untouched by my thought Process alone. God has bestowed upon me the gift of being lyrically inclined to speak to others through my words. So I will keep pouring my soul into pages and soothe my tears with my pen, hoping to enhance someone else's life through my journey." Welcome to 'LUTUS Under The Sun' the first of many more books presented by Troshell Richardson. Thank you for your support.

Contact Information...

www.blogspot.com/troshelld

www.facebook.com/shellyrichardson

www.instagram.com/Troshell Richardson

www.twitter.com/Shelly Richardson

For Booking:
Email: troshellr@gmail

Thank you all for your support. I am honored and grateful for the purchase of my book. Please feel free to send you comments to the email address listed above. Thanks again. Peace and many many Blessings.

www.ingramcontent.com/pod-product-compliance
Lightning Source LLC
Chambersburg PA
CBHW060426050426
42449CB00009B/2162